Faith in Society

Faith in Society

13 Profiles of Christians
Adding Value to the Modern World

ANTHONY B. BRADLEY

Foreword by Jordan J. Ballor

RESOURCE *Publications* · Eugene, Oregon

FAITH IN SOCIETY
13 Profiles of Christians Adding Value to the Modern World

Resource Publications
An Imprint of Wipf and Stock Publishers
199 W. 8th Ave., Suite 3
Eugene, OR 97401

www.wipfandstock.com

PAPERBACK ISBN: 978-1-5326-7209-5
HARDCOVER ISBN: 978-1-5326-7210-1
EBOOK ISBN: 978-1-5326-7211-8

Manufactured in the U.S.A.   JANUARY 10, 2019

To Dan Kunkle

Contents

Foreword

GOD'S RECLAMATION PROJECT

THE BASIC ELEMENTS OF the gospel message are familiar territory for most Christians. God created things good. Human beings fell into corruption and the rest of the world along with us. God's care for his creation led him to send help in the form of Jesus Christ. Jesus' life, death, and resurrection are the basis for the inbreaking of a new order, one in which "death shall be no more, neither shall there be mourning, nor crying, nor pain anymore, for the former things have passed away" (Rev 21:4 ESV).

It can be easy to think about such things in the abstract. We might even affirm them as true. But understanding them as real *for us* brings things to a whole other level. We might likewise believe that God is sovereign, all-powerful. But what do we make of the fact that this all-wise, all-knowing, all-powerful God became a human being, to live, suffer, die, and rise again? And why is there such a gap between Christ's resurrection and ascension and his second coming?

These are the kinds of concerns that go right to the heart of why there is human history at all. Christians believe that God is transcendent and utterly self-sufficient. In a radical sense, God needs nothing other than himself. So why is there anything at all? Theologians, philosophers, and everyday people have struggled with these questions for a long time, but the best answer is that

God, in his absolute and utter freedom, out of his liberality and love, chose gratuitously to create. And he didn't just create one thing; he created many things. He created *everything*.

When the integrity of that creation was compromised, he would have been entirely within his sovereign rights to renounce it. We get an idea of what a world without God's ongoing care and provision would look like in the depiction of the time before the Great Flood in Genesis 6: a veritable hell on earth. There's a sense in which to let things decay and return to the nothingness which evil strives for would have been just. "The wages of sin is death" (Rom 6:23 ESV).

But instead of abandoning his creation, corrupted and fallen though it was, God chose to remain faithful despite the unfaithfulness of what he had made. He decided to reclaim what had been taken away, and in this sense the gospel is all about God's reclamation project.

It is truly amazing to think of all the good things that God has done. As the apostle Paul continues, contrasting the fatal consequences of sin with God's grace, "the free gift of God is eternal life in Christ Jesus our Lord" (Rom 6:23 ESV). Even though humanity embraced sin and death, God has given creation the gift of new life. And along with that life, God has given us a purpose, a role to play in his reclamation project.

This too is something utterly gratuitous. God is all powerful. No doubt he can do whatever he desires to do as easily as he called everything into existence in the first place. But God has graciously deigned to give his fallible and frail human children some responsibilities in his larger work of redemption and reconciliation. And this is one of the places where the basic contours of the gospel really hits home with us. God has saved us, but he has saved us for a purpose. Yes, he has saved us for eternal life in Christ Jesus, but that eternal life already begins in some real sense right here, right now. God hasn't just saved us from death; he has saved us *for life*. He has saved us not only for ourselves, but also for others, and indeed, all of creation.

The Psalmist wonders, "When I look at your heavens, the work of your fingers, the moon and the stars, which you have set in place, what is man that you are mindful of him, and the son of man that you care for him?" He proceeds to answer, echoing the opening words of the Bible: "Yet you have made him a little lower than the heavenly beings and crowned him with glory and honor. You have given him dominion over the works of your hands; you have put all things under his feet, all sheep and oxen, and also the beasts of the field, the birds of the heavens, and the fish of the sea, whatever passes along the paths of the seas" (Ps 8:3–8 ESV).

God is concerned not only for human beings but also for all of creation. And he has placed humanity in a position of influence and responsibility, so that what we do matters not only for ourselves and for those around us, but indeed for everyone and everything.

If that sounds like a massive responsibility, that's because it truly is. But part of the good news is that God hasn't just picked us up and sent us on our way. He is here with us. He is radically present in the Holy Spirit. He gives us guidance through his Word. He has given us everything we need to be faithful children.

And the resources he has given us include our own abilities. God has given us reason, will, and emotion. And he wants us to use everything we have to serve him. The first great command as Jesus teaches us is to "love the Lord your God with all your heart and with all your soul and with all your mind and with all your strength" (Mark 12:30 ESV). God wants us to see things as he does and to care for them as he does.

God is so great, of course, that no single person, and indeed, all of humanity throughout history cannot encompass everything about him. So he uses each one of us, in our unique situations and with our unique sets of concerns, worries, relationships, and gifts to play a small part in his grand reclamation project and to reflect some aspect of his image in that work. If God is the master builder, we are some of the construction workers he has put into his service to restore his great temple.

This means that as wide and diverse as God's creation itself is, so too are his children called to serve faithfully across all of creation. There is work to be done in seeing God's will done in every area of our lives and in every aspect of existence. We have work to do in physics, mathematics, biology, and chemistry. We have responsibilities in music, painting, poetry, and literature. Christ taught us to pray for God's will to be done "on earth as it is in heaven" (Matt 6:10 ESV), and this is as true for the classroom and the dinner table as it is for the factory line and the church pew.

We might think of it this way. As Christians we have one calling: to faithfully follow Jesus Christ. But that single calling that all Christians share takes many different forms amidst the vagaries of human life and history. No single person on the planet alive today or at any point in human history has the same set of talents, relationships, dispositions, challenges, and possibilities as anyone you do. So while we all share a common calling as Christ's disciples, we have a unique responsibility to follow him in our own lives.

This is the kind of perspective on which the Christian university is founded. God's design encompasses all of creation, and so his servants need to be able to be equipped in a similarly universal and comprehensive way. This is also why there is a need for Christian institutions that are likewise focused on all kinds of different areas, throughout all of creation. Christians must work together to discover truths about the economy and implement just policy. Christians must be truth-tellers in the media and in journalism. We must be witnesses to beauty and goodness in music and the arts.

Jesus gives us the basic lesson in stewardship when he concludes that "Everyone to whom much was given, of him much will be required, and from him to whom they entrusted much, they will demand the more" (Luke 12:48 ESV). The stunning and glorious diversity of God's creation is manifest as well in the diversity of his church and those he has called to follow him. We have all been given much, but we haven't all been given the same things. As the apostle Paul puts it, "Now there are varieties of gifts, but the same Spirit; and there are varieties of service, but the same Lord; and there are varieties of activities, but it is the same God who empowers them all in everyone. To each is given the manifestation of the Spirit for the common good" (1 Cor 12:4–7 ESV).

God has given us new life in Jesus Christ, and that is very much indeed. He has given us a great deal, and so much is expected of each one of us. Each one of us is both an object and a subject of God's great reclamation project. He calls us and saves us from sin, death, and the Devil. But he calls us as well to serve him and to promote life and flourishing in this world.

Many church services have traditionally closed with the exhortation, "Go in peace. Serve the Lord." These two commands get at the heart of the gospel. We have peace because of what God has done for us. And on the basis of that peace we have been called and equipped to serve him throughout all of our lives and throughout all of creation. Thanks and praise be to God!

JORDAN J. BALLOR
The Acton Institute

Preface

ONE OF THE MOST stressful things high school and college students have to decide is "what they want to do for a living." In a country as wealthy and narcissistic as the United States, that question is particularly challenging because career has too often been reduced to a means of fulfilling oneself rather than a means of making the world the kind of place that reflects the reality of God by doing work that "destroys the devil's work" (1 John 3:8). The question of career choice for Christians would be much easier to discern if they were raised to look for the places where evil is flourishing and to choose a career path the seeks to fight evil and alleviate as much pain and suffering as possible. Instead, students are told to "do something they love" or "find a calling from God" (as if the Bible teaches that God's normative practice is to call individuals to particular jobs in the marketplace).[1] What is true, and challenging, is that students have innumerable options and the purpose of this book is to expand students' vision of what they might do with their lives in the future.

This book also intentionally challenges the notion that Christians doing the most provocative "Kingdom work" do so only in secular institutions and contexts. Too many young adults have been discouraged from working within Christian contexts because they've been unintentionally misled to believe that unless their work is directly related to influencing non-Christians it's less

---

1. By the way, the Bible does not teach that God's normative practice is to call individuals to particular jobs in the marketplace.

important to God's mission. One of the purposes of this book is to give Christian students permission to seek careers at Christian institutions and within Christian contexts because that work matters to God as well.

In this book we profile thirteen different Christian contexts available for Christians to explore because they intentionally want to work with other Christians for Christian purposes. What will be surprising to many is that, in college, a student can major in religious and theological studies oriented majors, with all sort of minors, and work in any of these contexts from business, to technology, to politics, and beyond. Being grounded in God's word and broad Christian theological and ethical traditions is the beginning of a great career in multiple contexts in the marketplace.

Acknowledgements

THIS BOOK IS A product of the many directions we help point students to at The King's College as we partner with other institutions in Christian Higher Education to graduate men and women who will advance the Kingdom of God on earth and is it in heaven. I would like to especially thank Phillip Reeves for his role as the principal researcher for this project and to my colleagues, staff, administration and the board of trustees at The King's College for their partnership in providing students vision for their preferred futures. The team at Wipf and Stock has always treated me with the highest level of professionalism and I am grateful for the work that Matt Wimer and Daniel Lanning did to make this book become a reality. Janet Wagner copy edited this book and she proved a fantastic set of fresh eyes for this project. Finally, I'd like to thank all the Christian high schools and quality homeschooling parents who are investing so much time integrating faith and learning before their students leave for university studies or the workforce after high school graduation.

1

Religion and Global Affairs

OVER THE PAST SEVERAL decades Christians from all over the world have been agents of human flourishing and mediators of religious discourse from across multiple religion traditions in an attempt to promote religious freedom and fight against religious persecution. Any country where the expression of any religion is repressed is a country where Christianity cannot thrive. As such, it's important for Christians to work hard to ensure that their religious tradition may be freely and fully expressed, and practiced like any other belief system. If you're serious about your own faith and religious freedom, working directly for a Christian organization involved in this work is a praiseworthy goal and one that could bring a lot of good in the world. Christian Solidarity Worldwide is one such organization, but there are many others around world. Of course, you could also start your own someday.

CHRISTIAN SOLIDARITY WORLDWIDE

The abuses started in 2016. Security forces for the civilian-led government in Burma began using extrajudicial measures to crack down on the ethnic Rohingya Muslims—their tactics: rape, torture, arson, and cold-blooded murder.[1] These efforts for "reform" resulted in hundreds of thousands of refugees, and other measures to crack down on those criticizing the authorities. With these abuses came atrocities against other minorities as well, often less well documented because their scope does not compare with the abuses against the Rohingya Muslims. Christian and Buddhist minorities have seen similarly brutal tactics from the military. A United Nations investigation found that two volunteer teachers with the Kachin Baptist Convention, both twenty years old, were raped and murdered, crimes that are apparently not isolated. The East Asia team leader for the Christian Solidarity Network, Benedicts Rogers, said that, "Burma as a whole requires urgent action," and described the situation as, "rapidly deteriorating."[2]

Churches and religious organizations have historically played a central role in healing these kinds of atrocities. This impact is largely seen in mercy ministries and outreaches, but it can encompass other spheres of international work as well. The ways that people and states relate have a direct impact on the billions of Christians in the Church globally and should be of great interest to those wishing to study the role of the Church in the contemporary world. Recently, the rise of Christian nonprofit organizations has brought this international focus of the Church into a new light, as many in the secular world are realizing the importance of faith-based nonprofits.

One such organization is Christian Solidarity Worldwide (CSW). The organization advocates for religious freedom, standing with and for the persecuted Church in over twenty countries throughout Asia, Africa, the Middle East, and Latin America. Religious freedom is one of the most violated human rights in the world—with three-quarters of the world's population living in countries with severe restrictions on religion.

CSW is working to change these numbers. Their mission and goals are broad and encompass elements in multiple spheres where they function as both advocates and educators of the global

1. Human Rights Watch, "Burma."
2. Smith, "Burmese Soldiers Accused."

Church and various governments and as encouragers of the persecuted. Over the last three decades, CSW has worked with the United Kingdom's Parliament, the United Nations, the European Union, and the United States Congress to provide accurate reports on the status of religious freedom worldwide. They work as educators, providing training on international human rights laws as they relate to religious freedom and abuses of this right.

Their team has delivered information and reports for government officials in each of the previously mentioned governing bodies and has even gained accreditation, or ECOSOC Consultative Status, at the United Nations in 2017. Their work at the United Nations has already shown promise, but it will now be more effective and timely as they can host their own side events. CSW's United Nations work so far has contributed to official inquiries in to human rights abuses in North Korea and Eritrea, with the organization making several statements each year to the United Nations Human Rights Council.

Christianity is central to CSW, where a statement of faith based on the Apostles' Creed and a scriptural foundation to their mission and vision guide their daily efforts. Part of their mission includes engaging churches worldwide to help pray for and encourage those experiencing persecution, imprisonment, and various trials. They offer practical support such as resources to write letters to those under house arrest for their faith and the ability to join campaigns for religious freedom.

CSW is headquartered in London, with offices in Washington, D.C., and Brussels, Belgium. Their leadership and board of directors consist of men and women from various spheres of church, government, education, and nonprofit leadership from around the world.

Majors That Get You Here:

Religious studies, with a minor in international affairs; political science, sociology, peace and conflict studies, international relations, and so on.

2

Religion, Business, and the Marketplace

IN THE FILM FOR *the Life of World*, viewers are introduced to the word *oikonomia*, which is one way of talking about God's economy of all things. That is, it's a way of looking at the goodness God has established within the various sectors of society so that His people can bless the world and contribute to the proper ordering of creation. For example, entrepreneurs have a huge role to play in setting the world right. The world of business is one of the greatest experiences of God's goodness to society, and Christians working in the world of business, with explicitly Christian worldviews and presuppositions, is an admirable goal and should be encouraged. It is perfectly honorable and celebratory to want to work within a Christian business environment to bring about God's blessings to the world. Yes, you don't have to work in the secular business space in order to honor God in the world of business. For those of you who want to be entrepreneurs, Praxis Labs is a wonderful example of an openly market-driven and distinctly Christian enterprise. Maybe you could start your own business someday as well!

PRAXIS LABS

The business world is where many of man's greatest ideas are brought to fruition. Christians often have a negative view of the business world because of the sometimes messy, cutthroat competition within business. However, this competition is often what drives the world's most successful people to their best ideas. While the negative aspects of the business world are unattractive to many believers, at its best, business provides an outlet for people to use their ideas, creative passions, and talents to positively affect those around them.

Praxis Labs is in the business of effecting this positive change, especially in the entrepreneurial and start-up space. They believe in a philosophy of "redemptive entrepreneurship," a phrase they coined to encapsulate the entrepreneur who "seeks to embody the Gospel in creating and building a venture that leaves a meaningful impact on the world."[1] Basically, they believe that if the Judeo-Christian view of the good life is different than the cultural narrative, then they as Christians should start companies that look different too.

Since business is fundamentally about creating, how can Christians not infuse their personal creations with their knowledge of their Creator? This combining of Christian values and ideals with creativity and determination makes Praxis Labs a powerhouse not only in its home base of New York City, but across the globe.

Here's how Praxis works. Their creative engine starts with looking for creative ideas and content in both current and future entrepreneurs.[2] To support these entrepreneurs, programs and events serve to build a supportive and collaborative network to give the entrepreneurs mentors and collaborators. These connections then begin to collaborate on their concepts and use Praxis' platforms to put their ideas into motion. Finally, these ideas

1. Praxis, website.
2. Ibid., "Our Vision."

become ventures that are guided and maintained through the Praxis core team.

But, wait, doesn't this still run the risk of well-intentioned Christians getting consumed by the secular, profit-driven business world? Not with Praxis Labs' model, which is based on the biblical narrative of creation, fall, redemption, and restoration. Having this biblical view going into establishing a start-up leads the founder to fundamentally orient the company around a model of service— the business exists to serve people, not to use them.

This was a model that a college junior named Natalie saw firsthand when she attended a Praxis summer conference.[3] Coming from a Christian college, Natalie had seen a lot of businesses that focused too heavily on success and lacked a good place for rest and keeping your priorities straight. This is not a problem with Praxis. Her biggest takeaway was how they focused on your faith permeating every aspect of your life. This Christian inspiration behind each business was evident to her, whether the company was a nonprofit focused on human trafficking or a notebook company.

Ultimately, Praxis believes that building your business should happen in a community, not in a vacuum. This community focus is what showed Natalie that Praxis truly locks in on how running a successful business is part of living your life for Christ. This creative community is built through several different programs such as the Praxis Mentors. These are 150 successful business founders who come along side of new Praxis ventures and provide guidance for entrepreneurs as they get started. Starting a business can be intimidating and seem like it might clash with a commitment to Christ. Yet, through Praxis Labs, this is a project built in community with a long-lasting love for Christ.

Majors That Get You Here:

Religious studies, with a minor in business; business administration; marketing; business management; accounting; international business, finance, and others.

3. Hustek, discussion with author.

3

Religion, Culture, and the Arts

AMONG THE MOST POWERFUL mediums of communication throughout all of human history are music and poetry. The Bible itself is replete with music and poetry, like the book of Psalms, that communicate the truths of God to his people and the world at large. It is perfectly legitimate, admirable, and honorable to want to produce music and poetry for God's people and the world at large. After all, there are about 2.2 billion Christians in the world who need to be reminded of what God says.[1] Humble Beast Records is a wonderful example of artists, musicians, and poets working together as a community to communicate the realities of the Kingdom of God to God's people and to the world.

HUMBLE BEAST

When Thomas Terry was first looking for a way to impact not just his community in Portland, Oregon, but the country as a whole, his first thought was to start a nonprofit.[2] But, he was pretty skeptical as to how many Christians would donate to a ministry of rappers.

1. World Atlas.
2. Humble Beast Records, "Humble Beast Becomes More Than Music."

Yes, Thomas wanted to start a hip-hop and spoken-word record label. Actually, Thomas is better known by his stage name Odd Thomas—he's a rapper. This put him in a tricky spot, since he and his potential directors didn't have the funds to just start this record label, but they still felt like the "creatives" in America were being completely overlooked by the church. Here's what made it even more interesting—Odd Thomas and his friend and potential co-founder Bryan Winchester (professionally known as Braille) were already signed to record labels. They didn't need a new label. They actually were each going to start their own record labels.[3] Yet, they saw an opportunity to do more than just be another record label, producing and profiting off of Christian artists. They saw a chance to start one joint record label to truly create a ministry that goes beyond just albums and reaches a new, different demographic.

This collaboration is how Humble Beast Records started in 2009.[4] Braille and Odd Thomas saw that a new approach was necessary to reach the creative hipsters who would buy the Gospel message, but didn't buy into the traditional presentation of this message. Wanting to reach this demographic helped to inform Humble Beast is distinguish by its four organizing principles: creativity, humility, theology, and doxology.[5] These distinctives set the music of Humble Beast's nine artists apart as they pursue successful rap, hip-hop, and spoken word careers. Creativity in music is often present, but humility, theology, and doxology are not usually as common.

Humility is seen in another of Humble Beast's bold aims—to always have its music be free.[6] Initially, this meant that Braille and Odd Thomas still kept other side businesses going since Odd Thomas still wasn't sure that Christians would substantially support a nonprofit full of rappers.[7] Yet, by 2015, they had cut ties with their other projects and Humble Beast went entirely

---

3. Daniels, "How Beautiful Eulogy United."

4. Ibid.

5. Humble Beast, "About."

6. Ibid., "Humble Beast Becomes More Than Music."

7. Ibid.

nonprofit. This step of faith reflected the success of records from Humble Beast, but also the label's creativity in finding other ways to support their mission of free music.

Beyond donations, the label is supported through conferences and coffee. In 2015, Humble Beast started Left Coffee Roasters. This extension of the company came along with their CANVAS Conference—a conference on theology and creativity—to add even more sustainability to the label and their goal of free music.[8] Left Coffee Roasters focuses on making craft coffee accessible while also spreading the word about the aims and ambitions of Humble Beast. While coffee is not on obvious extension of a record label, the CANVAS conference is clearly in line with Humble Beast's aims. The necessity of spending days diving into creativity and theology is clear, since they "have found that without theology, creativity wanders from its original significance and purpose; while without creativity, theology often becomes cold, distant, and futile."[9]

This importance on theology and doxology—praise—is what both ties Humble Beast together and sets it apart. Correct theology is so vital to the label that their staff contains not just producers and musicians, but pastors, including a director of doctrine.[10] Both of these distinctive aims are seen in the joyful tracks of artists such as Propaganda, Sho Baraka, and Beautiful Eulogy. These artists bring together doctrine, culture, and creativity in such a way that it's hard to imagine why Christian creatives would do anything but cling to this field.

Majors That Get You Here:

Religious studies with culture and fine arts minor, English, literature, creative writing, fine arts, communications, media studies, music, music education, music history, and others.

8. Ibid., "Humble Beast Introduces Left Roasters."

9. Canvas Conference, "About."

10. Humble Beast, "Humble Beast Becomes More Than Music."

4

Religion and Economic Liberty

THE WORLD IS A complicated place. We need people who are willing to sit down to do the research to help us think through what God's world should look like and what challenges face the fullest expression of human flourishing in a world that is broken and often disordered. Think tanks are organizations where scholars come together to research and write on particular issues or public policies and then to advocate for those in various spaces across society. Just because you're interested in politics doesn't mean you should be a politician. You can also work at a think tank and be very involved in national and international public policy discussions. There are many think tanks that wed the presuppositions of Christianity with the various public policy issues of our time. The Acton Institute is a fantastic model of what it looks like to be explicitly religious while thinking deeply about political, economic, and religious liberty.

ACTON INSTITUTE

What if the inability to vote for whom you want meant the inability to worship who you want? This is the question Lord Acton pondered in the mid-to late 1800s as he conducted a long career in politics. With his Catholic background, Acton was blocked from attending Cambridge University.[1] This was his first encounter with religion as a barrier to intellectual thought. He carried that encounter with him into politics and began to develop thoughts on how politics, economics, and religion can't be separated. He thought that any restraint on any of those aspects of life prevented man from thinking and being truly free in the other realms.[2] Therefore, Lord Acton spent his career promoting freedom in all aspects of life, since "liberty is the condition which makes it easy for conscience to govern."[3]

To follow in his footsteps, the Acton Institute was founded in Grand Rapids, Michigan, in 1990.[4] Their mission is to carry out Lord Acton's legacy—standing up for liberty and showing people that "the market can function only when people behave morally."[5] The Acton Institute was founded out of a need for a free market voice that still recognized that morality is essential to economics. This was in direct opposition to the traditional libertarian stance of the day, which also said that freedom is essential to a flourishing life, but relegated morality entirely to a relative, personal decision.

Countering the libertarian position began with the Acton Institute issuing ten core principles by which they operate: dignity of the person, social nature of the person, importance of social institutions, human action, sin, rule of law and the subsidiary role of government, creation of wealth, economic liberty, economic value, and priority of culture.[6] With a well-defined position in the world of free-market economics, the Acton Institute is able to produce publications, events, and research with no doubts about the foundation of their economic reasoning.[7]

1. Acton Institute, "Lord Acton."
2. Ibid.
3. Ibid., "About."
4. Ibid.
5. Ibid.
6. Ibid., "Mission."
7. Ibid., "About."

Their publications reflect a realization that most of America is not currently on board with free markets, Christianity, and definitely not with both of them. Acton Institute publications from their fellows cover social commentary, politics, religion, and economic policy. Even though the Acton Institute is focused specifically on free markets and religion, again, they realize that freedom has to flourish everywhere for it to flourish anywhere.

The Acton Institute's conferences, seminars, and dinners are yet more chances to engage a skeptical intellectual community in conversation.[8] Events are a chance for the academic community and regular everyday people to go to Grand Rapids and explore both why freedom and morality go hand in hand and why freedom is essential in all parts of life.

Yet, it is in the area of research where the Acton Institute has always made a significant contribution to economic discussion. The *Journal of Markets & Morality* is their flagship research activity. This is a nationally recognized academic journal that conducts research into specific issues of economic policy.[9] Acton's research arm also publishes books and supports research scholarships and grants to help put the discussion about morality and economics on as many college campuses as possible.

The Acton Institute has made a substantial difference in the world of economics by fighting back against Christians who wished to retreat from economics. By showing that there is a moral, Christian approach to free markets, the Acton Institute presented the country with a version of economics that is not immoral or rash, but rich in history and virtue. For this, the Acton Institute illustrates how essential understanding religion is to understanding markets.

Majors That Get You Here:

Religious studies with a minor in economics, economics, political economy, philosophy, political science, international business, and government.

8. Ibid., "Events."
9. Ibid., "Acton Research."

5

Religion and History

It is impossible to tell the story of Western civilization without directly explaining the role of Christianity and Christian institutions in the formation of the various principles that those in the West hold dear. Religious historians are a necessary part of telling the history of any aspect of Western society and, because of that, finding a job as a professional historian is a viable career direction. Church denominations are especially happy to have historians keep the story of their traditions alive. Presbyterian historical organizations in the United States and Ireland provide excellent models of what professional historians in the Church do for the Church and culture at large.

PRESBYTERIAN HISTORICAL SOCIETIES

When thinking on the founding of the United States, the term *Founding Fathers* usually inspires thoughts of George Washington, Benjamin Franklin, and Thomas Jefferson. Yet, there were many other Founding Fathers who were just as significant that most people have never heard of. Thankfully, there are historical societies who have fought to keep other Founding Fathers and their legacies alive in America's memory. One of those men is John

Witherspoon, the only man to sign the Declaration of Independence while being a Presbyterian minister.[1] His legacy and the role that his Presbyterian convictions played in his involvement in the War for Independence would have been forgotten if not for the Presbyterian Historical Society (PHS).

The PHS preserves the history of the Presbyterian Church of the USA (PCUSA) and the legacies of the denomination's most key members.[2] They tell the stories of past Presbyterians through preservation, exhibits, and publications.[3]

One of the easiest ways for Christianity to be devalued and misrepresented in today's world is if people do not actively try to preserve stories and memorabilia that unquestionably tell the truth of how things were. This preservation also brings stories to life and shows people the importance of history and tradition, not through boring details, but through putting them in the shoes of men and women who have walked before them. For the Historical Society, this takes the form of maintaining family trees, time lines, and lists of historical sites.[4]

For those who want to preserve the visuals of history, the Historical Society curates exhibits online, in print, and in person.[5] These exhibits highlight the PCUSA's musical traditions, artifacts from various mission fields, and the denomination's role in different wars and key social moments.[6]

For literature, they've published a journal since 1901 that is currently known as the *Journal of Presbyterian History*, even though it has had five different names previously.[7] In tandem with this is the *Presbyterian Heritage*, the denomination's biannual print newsletter.

---

1. Independence Hall, "Presbyterian Historical Society."
2. Presbyterian Historical Society, "About."
3. Ibid., "History Online."
4. Ibid.
5. Ibid.
6. Ibid., "Exhibits," Presbyterian Historical Society.
7. JSTOR, "Presbyterian Historical Society."

Across the pond, the Presbyterian Historical Society of Ireland is also a strong resource for those wanting to research the Presbyterian Church and build on past studies. The history of Presbyterianism in Ireland is especially interesting since it captured three different veins of the denomination blending them to become one.[8] The Irish Society's large archives of bulletins, sermon transcripts, family trees, and clerical documents allows for the conducting of countless research projects. From this, historians can use theological training to build a story of how Presbyterianism came to America, or maybe a story of how the denomination thrived in spite of famine in Ireland in the 1800s. Without a proper understanding of theology, church history is only seen as just that—history. But, when a historian can truly understand the decision process of the people being studied, it brings documents to life and reveals a story of the preservation of religion.

History takes on many forms. Whether it is written word, spoken word, or words brought to life, a Christian with a love of history can combine their faith with their love of history. Organizations like the Presbyterian Historical Society allow for Christians to fully embrace their faith while using their skills in historical discovery, analysis, and preservation to explore even more about the history of what they believe.

Majors That Get You Here:

Religious studies with a history minor, library science, history, historical preservation, and others.

---

8. Presbyterian Historical Society of Ireland, "About Us."

6

Religion and International Business

GOD'S PEOPLE OPERATING AND running successful businesses is as
old as the Pentateuch. Some Christians believe that it is culturally
transformative to be a "behind-the-scenes" Christian where your
Christian presuppositions are hidden in the marketplace in such a
way that people have to *discover* that your business was operating
with Christian principles. It is also perfectly honorable and admirable to put your Christian presuppositions at the forefront of your
business practices for everyone to see. While Chick-fil-a is one of
the most well-known examples, the fashion industry has examples
in companies like Forever 21, which operates more than 815 stores
in fifty-seven countries, including the United States, Australia,
Brazil, Canada, China, France, Germany, Hong Kong, India, Israel,
Japan, Korea, Latin America, Mexico, Philippines, and the United
Kingdom.[1]

FOREVER 21

Where is the line between the beliefs of a company and the beliefs
of the people running the company? Today, it's very common for

1. Chen, "Forever 21."

businesses, especially large international brands, to act like morally neutral organizations that cloak what their employees' individual beliefs are. This is in an attempt to make the brand appeal to as many people as possible and make everyone feel as if the company is designed specifically for them. However, Forever 21 took a different, attention-grabbing approach to being an international brand.

Started in 1984 in California by the Chang family from South Korea, Forever 21 took the United States retail market by storm, selling desirable clothes at rock-bottom prices—their most expensive item is only sixty-five dollars.[2] As new immigrants to the country, the Changs quickly saw a problem in the American clothing market—nice designer clothes were too expensive for middle class Americans. The Changs had not previously run a major business, but with only $11,000 to their name and a strong belief in a clear business model, they opened the first Forever 21 in a small 900 square-foot storefront in Los Angeles.[3] This simple business model—produce efficiently, give items a designer look, and sell as cheaply as possible—took off so quickly that after its first year, Forever 21 opened a new store every six months.[4]

Their success, with the company worth approximately $3 billion in 2011 and stores on multiple continents, is not the only eye-catching part of the business.[5] The Changs are devout Christians, putting an importance on faith and family that is rare in the realm of international business. For Christians in business, it is always tricky to know how your faith will be received by business partners and if you should even make your faith readily apparent as part of your company. Forever 21 has directly addressed the question of how to be an incredibly successful international business while not shying away from the role of faith in the company.

Forever 21 went with an overall subtle approach to integrating faith with business, but it was still a more forward approach

2. Wiseman, "The Gospel According to Forever 21."

3. *Forbes*, "Profile: Do Won & Jin Sook Chang."

4. Ibid.

5. Wiseman, "The Gospel According to Forever 21."

than most other businesses. In the last few years, the brand has come under fire for printing the Bible reference John 3:16 on the bottom of their shopping bags and Mr. Chang keeping a Bible open on his desk.[6] Are these two simple acts crossing the line when it comes to the world of business?

If the verdict comes from the cash register, then the answer is an emphatic no. The company has continued to be worth over $3 billion despite the public questioning of the Changs' faith, with the store even expanding to more countries.[7] But, if the company is so successful, why risk upsetting your customers by bringing religion into the mix? For Mr. Chang, it wasn't really a choice to make. "I hoped others would learn of God's love. So that's why I put it there," said Mr. Chang.[8]

This optimism, given to Mr. Chang through his faith, is a key driver of the success of his business. He is using the platform he has to simply tell people, "Here is where my hope and optimism personally and professionally come from." It is this ability to look forward that gave him the ability to act on his bold business idea over thirty years ago. It is this same optimism that pushes him to expand the brand while not shying away from the fact that it is his faith and not his finances, which gives his life meaning and purpose.

Majors That Get You There:

Religious studies, with a minor in business; business administration; marketing; business management; accounting; international business, finance, and others.

6. McGregor, "Forever 21's Leaked Memo."
7. *Forbes*, "Profile: Do Won & Jin Sook Chang."
8. CNN, Do Won Chang interview.

7

Religion and Journalism

CHRISTIANS ARE PEOPLE OF the truth. Christians live the truth and speak the truth in love. Again, the world is a complicated place, and Christians have a role to play in helping each other understand God's world using distinctly Christian presuppositions at the outset. For some, reporting the news should not be any different. While it's wonderful to be a journalist who is a Christian doing quality work in secular newsrooms, it is also perfectly admirable and honorable to report the news from explicitly Christian presuppositions about the world to help Christians discern what's happening in the world and for the world to see that Christians really do see the world in unique ways. As mentioned earlier, with 2.2 billion Christians in the world, there is a role for Christians to report the truth about what's happening in the ways that point to opportunities for applications of the gospel. WORLD News Group is but one example of Christianity's rich news reporting history.

WORLD NEWS GROUP

When L. Nelson Bell saw a concerning tendency toward nontraditional theology in the 1940s, he decided the best way to foster support against this trend was to start a magazine. He and a local minister started the *Southern Presbyterian Journal*, which over the next decade became nationally known for traditional doctrine and accurate reporting on the path of the Southern Presbyterian denomination.[1] In the '70s and '80s when the PCA split from the ever more liberal PCUSA, Bell's journal was left in flux. The journal's board started publishing a children's paper around this time that left adults begging for a Christian magazine for adults on world affairs. So, in 1986, *WORLD Magazine* began.

What set *WORLD* apart was that it wasn't just high-quality Christian journalism, but high-quality journalism—period.[2] The magazine continues to stand out today because of its core commitment to Christian truth. In a world that is always searching for the meaning of truth, few news organizations have an objective sense of truth to which they are committed. This gives its journalism a degree of consistency for readers to expect. Standing true to the reason for its founding, *WORLD* tackles the more controversial topics in the world since those are the issues that have the greatest impact on the future of both religion and politics.

WORLD is also innovative within the Christian journalism arena. As the Internet developed in the late '90s, *WORLD* quickly embraced the new means of communication to increase distribution.[3] Combining this with their radio advertisement innovations in the previous decade, *WORLD* set itself apart within Christian news circles as the highest quality publication based on Christian principles. Even as *WORLD* continued to put itself on the level of secular magazines, it also wanted to be recognized as a distinctly Christian magazine.

WORLD takes a holistic approach to journalism—reporting on all areas and not shying away from news topics traditionally viewed as outside of the concerns of Christians. Focusing on the arts, economics, technology, and more, *WORLD* has an underlying concern for human dignity and virtue that doesn't make its way into traditional news outlets. With this has also come

1. *Forbes*, "Do Won & Jin Sook Chang."
2. Belz, "Publishing . . . by Design."
3. Ibid.

nationally recognized investigative reporting on stories in the Christian world. In 2009, *WORLD* led the way in exposing the C Street House in Washington, D.C., a scandal clouded in twisted theology and infidelity from politicians.[4] With this level of critical journalism, *WORLD* was applauded within the journalism community for its commitment to honest journalism, even when investigating fellow Christians.[5]

The end result is a publication that shows that quality journalism is inherently compatible with Christianity. In a world where the media keeps marginalizing Christians more and more, *WORLD* stands apart with a simultaneous commitment to Christian principles and rigorous reporting. With *WORLD* showing how Jesus and journalism are easily intertwined, the magazine stands as a leader pushing Christian journalism to be the most articulate example for Christ it can be.

Majors That Get You Here:

Religious studies with a minor in journalism, communications, journalism, political science, history, English, sociology, international relations, government, media studies, and others.

4. Belz and Pitts, "All in the family."
5. Horton, "Reporting on C Street."

8

Religion and Literature

THE WORLD NEEDS GOOD writers and good stories that point people to the truth. It seemed appropriate for this profile to highlight the life and work of C.S. Lewis as a sort of "jazz standard" for how this could be done. Lewis's fiction and nonfiction essays are among the best from Western Christianity and the legacy of his work will extend for generations to come. The world needs more Christians who have a deep knowledge of the Bible and theology but also have imaginations that invite a sense of awe and wonder about the truth. C.S. Lewis was a writer without equal in this category.

C.S. LEWIS

What is the key to books having long-lasting influence? We all read every day, but certain books and authors have a seemingly inexplicable ability to hook generation after generation. Look at C.S. Lewis. His books have sold over 200 million copies worldwide and continue to sell well today even though he passed away over fifty years ago.[1] The key to this long-term influence is that Lewis combined religion with literature in a compelling way that ad-

---

1. Smith, "C.S. Lewis."

dressed man's need to find insight to the meaning of life. Lewis told Christian truths alongside his own life struggles to create engaging books that captured the imagination of anyone, young or old.

Lewis declared himself an atheist shortly after leaving boarding school as a teenager.[2] Yet, once he met J.R.R. Tolkien, who was already a Christian, Tolkien began intellectual sparring on the battlefield of Lewis's heart over their difference in eternal destination. After three years of this sparring, Lewis turned from atheism to theism, acknowledging God's existence, but not acknowledging him as Savior.[3] Two years later, Lewis and Tolkien took a late-night stroll to discuss spiritual matters. Not long after that, Lewis wrote these words to a friend: "I have just passed on from believing in God to definitely believing in Christ . . . My long night talk with . . . Tolkien had a great deal to do with it".[4] This conversion from atheism gave Lewis the ability to write empathetically to non-believers since he had once been in their shoes.

The depth of Lewis's work is also strengthened by his own experiences with death. While serving in WWI, Lewis was part of the Battle of the Somme, which had more than a million casualties.[5] This experience with immense suffering came on the heels of losing his mom as a young boy. After the war, Lewis's first wife, Joy, passed away from bone cancer just a few years after their marriage, leaving Lewis to care for her two teenage sons.[6] This great amount of personal loss gave him the ability to write stories and poems in more than ten different genres, including literary criticism, fairy tales, monologues, and science fiction. He excelled particularly at taking the imagination on vivid journeys in fairy-tales like *The Chronicles of Narnia*. It would have been undeniably unnatural for Lewis to segregate his faith from his writing, so even his children's books like *The Chronicles of Narnia* are infused with biblical allusions. The universality of his message is why even the

2. Blake, "Surprised by C.S. Lewis."
3. Monda, "The Conversion Story of C.S. Lewis."
4. Ibid.
5. Vincent, "C.S. Lewis Facts."
6. C.S. Lewis College, "C.S. Lewis."

fairytales of *Narnia* have sold more than 100 million copies in more than forty languages.[7] On the opposite end of the spectrum, *Mere Christianity* is nonfiction and based primarily on Lewis's radio shows during World War II, and yet, *Mere Christianity* is a regular in America's top-fifty religious books with annual sales of 250,000 copies.[8]

Lewis's influence through literature is undeniable. This happened even though he had no official office of leadership and was even passed over for promotion in the world of academia because of his Christian beliefs.[9] But, he did not seek the spotlight; he simply sought to share the healing he found in Christ through his conversion and encounters with death with those who were hurting just like he was. The result is an author who more than half a century after his death is still able to guide anyone who doubts Christ toward the truth.

Majors That Get You Here:

Religious studies with a literature minor, English, literature, history, creative writing, classics, and the humanities.

---

7. Erlanger, "Chronicles of C.S. Lewis."

8. Ibid.

9. C.S. Lewis College, "C.S. Lewis."

9

Religion and Media Studies

IT'S BECOME THE NORM to mock Christian filmmakers for producing low-quality and uninspiring programs. Much is warranted but instead of settling for mockery a better approach would be to invest resources in raising a generation of Christian filmmakers and media production company employees who want to lead with their Christian presuppositions and commitments to add value not only to the Kingdom of God but to society at large. Christians in the media have a unique opportunity to point everyone to the truth and it's perfectly admirable and honorable to seek to produce distinct content that intersects with Christianity in a way, for example, that mirrors the wisdom literature in the Bible, and acts as an in invitation to think about the nature of reality that points to transcendental, cosmic truth. Magic Lantern Pictures provides an outstanding model of what it means to make everyone think about the truth whether they are Christians or not.

MAGIC LANTERN PICTURES

Spring Break is one of the supposed high points of a college student's time at university. It's promoted as a time to truly let loose and indulge all your senses. Most students act like this is the ultimate fulfillment of their desires as it lets them liberate themselves from all pressures around them. But, what if your exploits were recorded and you were put face to face with your own approach to drinking, sex, and freedom?

Magic Lantern Pictures recognizes the power that can come from taking everyday situations, putting them on film, and showing a narrative that either people had not previously realized or chose to ignore. It would have been simple for Magic Lantern to become one of many documentary studios and not really stand out. But, what sets them apart, especially in the realm of filmmakers who are Christians, is the almost Socratic method of storytelling the studio uses. Magic Lantern's main directors and producers Benjamin Nolot, Morgan Perry, and SJ Murray are Christians, but their landmark documentary, *Liberated: The New Sexual Revolution*, is not explicitly Christian at face value.[1]

Instead of going to Panama City Beach and telling everyone they want to explore the topic of sex from a Christian perspective that views people as more than just sex toys, they simply ask questions. They follow a handful of students around during Spring Break, asking them about the different situations they find themselves in. Through this approach, Magic Lantern makes the Christian viewpoint on human worth and sex very clear, while using a manner of presentation that people from all religious backgrounds could accept.

The choice to use film to bring this important conversation to the mainstream table came from Magic Lantern's parent organization, Exodus Cry, a nonprofit committed to fighting sex trafficking.[2] Exodus Cry had already seen success in traditional methods that Christians have used to combat sex trafficking. But, they realized that using the creative visual arts would be the best way to communicate the harmful everyday views on sex that ultimately lead to these massive industries that everyone easily sees as evil.

This is where Magic Lantern is truly making an impact in the world. Because of this Christian backing, it gives the studio a

1. Wise, "Netflix Teams with Christian Group."
2. Exodus Cry, "About."

unique and theologically inspired view on human dignity.[3] This leads them to find subjects that can work as a canvas to present their mission and values. A values-first approach to filmmaking is unique in an industry that is widely criticized for lacking a moral basis for many marque films. But, through Magic Lantern, organizations like Exodus Cry have been able to use film to promote messages of dignity and worth that stand out positively in the arts and might otherwise have been ignored.

Majors That Get You Here:

Religious studies with a media studies minor, media studies, film, fine arts, communications, sociology, history, psychology, and others.

3. Magic Lantern Pictures, "You've Seen Liberated."

10

Religion and Philosophy

PHILOSOPHY HAS HAD A challenging relationship with Christian theology since the Enlightenment. In general, Western philosophy that does not presuppose the reality of the Triune God, from a Christian perspective, is a framework that seeks to give an account of reality as if God does not exist. If God does not exist, the human person is an autonomous being whose existence is without a framework or destination. Rejecting the existence of God through philosophy over centuries created wonderful opportunities for thoughtful Christians to provide a defense of the Christian faith by listening well and answering people's questions. The study of philosophy is vital to understanding how to provide an explanation of the Christian faith with empathy, patience, and love. There is a great need for Christians to study philosophy because they want to use it to serve the Church and aid in defending the faith. My friend Jared is completing a PhD in philosophy at Texas A&M University. He says philosophy is important because you use philosophy when explaining your faith anyway. "Every time you argue for something, you're participating in the relationship between ideas and how they are used. Studying philosophy is one way to see which ideas and their relationships can be more helpful and more clear," said Jared. One model of integrating philosophy to listen well and ask good questions was the international ministry of Francis and Edith Schaeffer called "L'Abri."

L'ABRI FELLOWSHIP

Amelia grew up Christian through and through.[1] Her dad was a pastor, and she was raised in Tennessee, the heart of the Bible Belt. But, like so many teenagers, when she went to college, she had to make her parents' worldview her own. Yet, the people she met and the academics from whom she learned left her questioning if Christianity could hold its ground intellectually. Without someone to really give a logical, philosophical, and intellectual account of Christianity, Amelia questioned if her faith would last.

Decades earlier, Apologist Francis Schaeffer recognized this need that Amelia and countless people before her had also had. Seminaries and churches were great, yet what about those who didn't feel called to seminary but still had a deep need for strong intellectual conversation on Scripture? In response to this, in 1955 Francis and his wife, Edith, opened up their home in Switzerland as a lodge where Christians could come live with them for a few months and address the questions about Christianity that threatened to push them away from Christ.[2]

They called it *L'Abri*, French for shelter.[3] What set the Schaeffers apart is that L'Abri focused on addressing the practical questions of Christianity in community away from the heart of bustling cities. They built L'Abri on a strong Reformed mission and values.[4] They began with the belief that Christianity "is objectively true and that the Bible is God's written word to mankind."[5] This makes the Bible rationally compatible with the world around us. Because Christianity is rational, it addresses the whole world and there is

1. Worthen, "Not Your Father's L'Abri."
2. L'Abri, "History."
3. Ibid.
4. Ibid.
5. Ibid.

not just a part of life called the Christian realm for which it is relevant. This pushes Christians to be truly human instead of trying to get to an impossible to reach spiritual plane. Since this requires recognizing that everyone is broken and needs to come to these conversations from that place of human brokenness, both intellectuals and non-intellectuals were essential to the dialogue at L'Abri.

This model quickly caught on and uncovered a widespread, international need for a new philosophical way to present the Gospel. Over the last fifty years, L'Abri has expanded from one location to ten, reaching every continent except Antarctica.[6] The Schaeffer's bold belief that God's word was not just Christian truth but "true truth" led to both Christians and non-Christians going to L'Abri.[7] Today, this means that L'Abri, especially its locations in America, have a strong draw not just for skeptics, but for those who feel their evangelical upbringing didn't truly convince them about Christ.[8] Yet, since the Schaeffers established their ministry with those four strong teachings on the truth of Scripture, L'Abri was able to easily adapt to the changing doubts of their visitors.

By retreating into nature, L'Abri is able to have strong philosophical discussions on the ability of Christianity to reach and change all aspects of culture while removing visitors from the stress and strains of urban and suburban life. Since each L'Abri house has multiple visitors at a time, a small community is formed. This strengthens the philosophical pursuit going on in the house, since this small community is meant to be a replica of daily life instead of feeling like you've left the world to go sit in a classroom. By setting the discussion in this social and communal context, visitors are easily able to transition back to normal life without feeling like their knowledge from L'Abri is now lost by having to apply it in regular social interactions.

People come to accept Christ for many different reasons. People also are sustained in their faith by different means, whether emotional, relational, or intellectual connections. L'Abri saw a

6. Ibid.

7. Bars, "The Beginnings of L'Abri, II."

8. Worthen, "Not Your Father's L'Abri."

strong need to counter the mainstream intellectual community's message that Christianity is only for the simpleminded. By infusing theological teachings with rich discussions on philosophy, L'Abri became a ministry that both brings skeptics to Christ and strengthens the faith of those who thought of walking away.

Majors That Get You Here:

Religious studies with a philosophy minor, apologetics, theology, biblical studies, philosophy, history, sociology, and others.

11

Religion and Politics

CHRISTIANS SHOULD BE INVOLVED in the political spaces of the countries they inhabit in order to be citizens who contribute to the common good. Christian involvement in politics, however, should not be to attempt to turn secular governments into arms of the church, but the world of politics is place where you can leverage your influence to make a contribution to human flourishing. One of the best contemporary examples of Christian involvement with politics was the way the black church rallied to end Jim Crow rule in the South and to dismantle the evils of racial segregation. Christians differ on Christian involvement in politics, but the Ethics and Public Policy Center in Washington, D.C., is a good place for politically interested Christian students to begin thinking about these issues.

ETHICS AND PUBLIC POLICY CENTER

In 1976, Dr. Ernest Lefever saw a nation in the middle of the Cold War that was struggling to find a strong moral backbone in the realm of politics.[1] This was very hard for Lefever to see, as it was

---

1. Ethics and Public Policy Center, "About."

his belief in a strong moral system guiding the international order that led him away from pacifism. He grew up a pacifist, becoming a minister in the Church of Brethren, until he saw Europe after WWII.[2] Viewing the destruction that totalitarian governments brought to their own people convinced Lefever that pacifism could not be defended if he believed in a moral tradition that needed to be combined with politics.

Historically in the United States, religious morals were regularly considered alongside public policy. Presidents from George Washington to John F. Kennedy were openly Christian. To continue the integration of morals into public policy, Dr. Lefever started the Ethics and Public Policy Center (EPPC). The EPPC's goal is to apply "the Judeo-Christian moral tradition to critical issues of public policy."[3] They aim at this goal through nine programs designed to address aspects of public policy that the Center sees as requiring both moral and political insight. These programs keep the Center relevant in almost every political discussion as the programs cover bioethics, the Constitution, economics, health care, and more.[4]

One of the ways the EPPC goes about having discussions on policy and morality is through the speaking and writing of their twenty-four scholars. Instead of writing content primarily published by the EPPC, the scholars write for other publications like the *Wall Street Journal* and the *National Review*, and are regularly on major channels such as CNN and Fox News.[5] By bringing the discussion to as many Americans as possible, the EPPC hopes to illustrate that morality is not a secondary topic to public policy, but that the two must always be considered in tandem.

Another less frequently covered side of public policy the EPPC is actively involved in is with specifically religious issues. The EPPC regularly makes itself a key voice on issues involving free speech and Christianity, terrorism and Islam, and Israel and Judaism. They do this primarily through their Faith Angle

2. Bernstein, "Ernest W. Lefever Dies."

3. Ethics and Public Policy Center, "About."

4. Ibid., "Programs."

5. Ibid., "Fellows and Scholars."

Forum.[6] This branch of the EPPC aims to increase the amount of quality journalism and discussion in regards to religious topics.[7]

Through the EPPC, a focus on religion is allowed to flourish in a variety of ways. With the EPPC's foundation of habitually combining morality and politics, a deep understanding of historical Christianity is essential. With a solid grasp of this, scholars and journalists are able to effectively integrate themselves in Washington and speak up for the necessity of morality in all policy decisions.

Majors That Get You Here:

Religious studies with a politics minor, government, political science, political economy, history, international affairs, and others.

6. Faith Angle Forum.
7. Ibid., "About."

12

Religion and the Law

THERE ARE MANY GOOD reasons to go to law school to become a lawyer. Lawyers play a vital role in making civil society function properly. Lawyers help advance the cause of justice in so many areas of society. Unfortunately, some narrow approaches reduce the practice of law to a means to a comfortable life with social prestige rather than an opportunity to use law as a means of making the world a better place. International Justice Mission provides a wonderful model of practicing law for others.

INTERNATIONAL JUSTICE MISSION

When Gary Haugen joined the United States Department of Justice, he didn't imagine that the defining moment of his career would happen in Rwanda instead of in the United States. Soon after Gary started at the Justice Department in 1994 as a human rights attorney, he was loaned to the United Nations to head up their investigation of the mass genocide in Rwanda.[1] Going town to town and grave to grave permanently changed Gary. This investigation

---

1. International Justice Mission, "Get to Know Us."

opened his eyes to the urgent need of the poor not simply for food and shelter but to be protected.[2]

While the Rwandan genocide highlighted how prevalent violent oppression is, this kind of oppression of the helpless had been happening in many countries for many years. This discovery inspired Gary to start the International Justice Mission (IJM), "a group that would leverage the skills of criminal justice professionals to protect the poor from violent oppression."[3]

One of the biggest barriers to IJM's ability to protect the helpless has been government structures or a lack of them. While IJM's seventeen field offices are found in more than just developing countries, many of the countries they work in lack the adherence to the rule of law necessary to provide basic protection to the vulnerable. Other countries such as Canada and the United Kingdom are highly developed countries, but still lack the infrastructure and laws to provide a safety net for the vulnerable. To operate effectively regardless of which country IJM is currently in, they employ "lawyers, social workers, investigators, community activists, and other professionals."[4]

This barrier becomes even trickier to navigate when considered in IJM's primary realm of ending slavery. This is not just sex slavery; it's anything involving "the use of lies or violence to force another person to work for little or no pay."[5] Slavery is banned in virtually every country, but without proper enforcement, bondage is still rampant, trapping 40 million people worldwide.[6] This lack of enforcement is part of the cycle of poverty that caught many of these victims in slavery to begin with.

IJM uses a data-driven approach to work with local governments to identify rescue areas and coordinate with local courts to make sure that rescuing victims goes hand in hand with

2. Ibid.
3. Ibid.
4. Ibid.
5. Ibid., "Slavery."
6. Ibid.

prosecuting their oppressors.[7] However, IJM is not merely reactionary; their legal team also works with governments to build up sustainable ways for each nation to identify how they can prevent slavery before and after IJM goes to a country.

IJM's Christian foundation is in direct contrast to the exploitation that is the driving force behind slavery. It would be one thing for a social justice organization or a government to take on the issue of slavery. But, what if the human problems underlying the causes of slavery are not also addressed? Many of the victims wonder how God can be real if he allows them to suffer in this slavery without any rescue. When IJM saves one of the 40,000 people they have saved to date, they are able to say that God is real and that his example is why IJM has come to free the oppressed.

Majors That Get You Here:

Religious studies with a philosophy minor, government, political science, political economy, history, international affairs, philosophy, pre-law studies, and others.

7. Ibid., "Who We Are."

13

Religion and Technology

THE OPPORTUNITIES TO ADD value to the world through technological innovation are almost endless. Christians who are paying
attention to the needs of the world and are skilled at creating quality technological products will be the business and community
leaders of the future. The intersection of meeting real needs with
technological innovation, with Christian presuppositions in hand,
is a real asset to the world. The need for innovation that serves
the ongoing work of the Christian institutions is needed as well.
It's perfectly admirable and honorable to use your gifts, interests,
imagination, and technical skills to serve the needs of the Church.
The team at Faith Street did just that!

FAITH STREET

When Sean Coughlin moved to New York City in 2011, he was
surprised by how hard it was to find key information on different
churches in the city.[1] In a city as tech-savvy as New York, this
lack of good information seemed like a major oversight. How were
people supposed to find the right church for them out of the over

1. Ericksen interview by Reeves.

2,000 churches in New York City?[2] So, Shaun took matters into his own hands and created Faith Street, a company that now serves as a directory for approximately 85 percent of churches nationwide.[3] Sean's co-founder, Glenn Ericksen, sees Faith Street as a great way to have technology not only intersect with faith, but truly help people become more rooted in their faith through connecting them with a church community.

Glenn has a background in church planting and is the technology brains behind Faith Street. Initially, he was a bit wary of getting involved with a start-up since he knew that start-ups—especially in New York—required round-the-clock devotion to the company, making it impossible to keep a Sabbath. Yet, this is where his theology background played a big role in his decision to help found Faith Street. With a deeper understanding of Scripture's teachings on work and rest, he saw that his identity was not found in his work and not found in how successful his start-up is. Therefore, if his work was not his identity, it made sense to allow himself to rest along with pursuing success. With this biblically informed mentality, Glenn and Sean were able to establish a tech company that allows Christians to search for the right church for them based on the vibe, time, denomination, and programs offered. The church directory allows for churches to truly be accessible communities that are very upfront with potential members about what to expect and how to get meaningfully plugged-in.

Once Faith Street became established as a reputable and well-known church directory, churches came to Sean and Glenn with another problem—how can tithing be made easier? Churches from all across the country expressed to them that giving is a "higher friction process," as Glenn puts it.[4] Initially, they were a bit surprised with this request since the narrative they had heard over the last few years was that churches weren't really interested in technology. This was wrong. It wasn't that churches didn't want tech; there just wasn't any good technology out there for tithing

2. Curan, "Churches Are Now Accepting Donations Through Apps."

3. Ericksen interview by Reeves.

4. Ibid.

specifically. Even though digital giving was very different than Faith Street's current tech offering, they decided to run with this second branch of the company since it fit with their overall aim of removing barriers within the Church.

Once again Sean's and Glenn's theological backgrounds were vital. In the modern world, tech companies constantly pitch their products as a way for technology to save us from whatever is around us. Faith Street views technology, not as a savior, but as a way to "nudge people to better practices and better systems," says Glenn.

With another barrier removed for churches, this relationship between technology and faith allows for churches to focus on preaching the Gospel, building community, and redeeming creation. When the potential for technology to help churches innovate and simplify the tasks they need to achieve is recognized, it puts a historical church in a modern context while improving its ability to succeed.

Majors That Get You Here:

Religious studies with minors in innovation, technology, and design; web design, information science, computer science, graphic design, computer engineering, computer programming, design and visual communications, and others.

Conclusion

MANY HIGH SCHOOL AND college students mistakenly believe that their college major determines what their career will be in the future. It does not by necessity. People in business like Peter Thiel, Carl Icahn, Carly Fiorina, Gerald Levin, and many others, were all philosophy majors in college. Religion and religious studies majors gave us people like Richard Searer, president of the American division of Kraft Foods, Inc., David Chang the famous founder of the Momofuku restaurant group, and former FBI director James Comey, Jr. In fact, not only do religious studies majors score significantly higher than political science majors on the Law School Admissions Test (LSAT), but international affairs and non-profit work are common destinations for those studying the intersection of religion and culture. As such, college majors don't equal jobs and colleges are not merely job training centers. As a Christian college student, you will be in school to discover as much about yourself and God's world as possible. You will be on campus to be shaped intellectually, morally, spiritually, and emotionally so that you are equipped to be "salt and light" in a broken world. Think about it this way: in the book of Daniel, what did Daniel and his friends study in order to have careers in the government of the Babylonians? Go back and read the first six chapters. The answer may surprise you. In conclusion, major in something that challenges you to learn new things about God's world and God will place you where you're needed later.

Bibliography

Acton Institute. "About." Accessed June 25, 2018. https://acton.org/about.
———. "Acton Research." Accessed June 25, 2018. https://acton.org/research/about-acton-research.
———. "Events." Accessed June 25, 2018. https://acton.org/events.
———. "Lord Emerich Edward Dalberg Acton." July 20, 2010. https://acton.org/lord-emerich-edward-dalberg-acton.
———. "Our Mission and Core Principles." Accessed June 25, 2018. https://acton.org/about/mission.
Bars, Jerram. "The Beginnings of L'Abri, II," Covenant Seminary. Spring 1990. https://www.covenantseminary.edu/resources/wp-content/uploads/sites/5/2014/12/CC579_T_02.pdf.
Belz, Emily and Edward Lee Pitts. "All in the Family." WORLD. August 14, 2009. https://world.wng.org/2009/08/all_in_the_family.
Belz, Joel. "Publishing . . . by Design." WORLD News Group. March 24, 2001. https://world.wng.org/2001/03/publishing_by_design.
Bernstein, Adam. "Ernest W. Lefever Dies at 89." LA Times, July 31, 2009. http://www.latimes.com/local/obituaries/la-me-ernest-lefever31-2009jul31-story.html.
Blake, John. "Surprised by C.S. Lewis: Why His Popularity Endures." CNN, December 17, 2010. http://religion.blogs.cnn.com/2010/12/17/surprised-by-c-s-lewis-why-his-popularity-endures/.
Canvas Conference. "About." Accessed June 25, 2018. http://www.thecanvasconference.com/about/.
Chang, Do Won. Interview by CNN, CNN, September 21, 2012. http://transcripts.cnn.com/TRANSCRIPTS/1209/21/ta.01.html.
Chen, I-Chun. "Forever 21 Expanding F21 Red Concept to 40 New Locations. Accessed October 8, 2018. https://www.bizjournals.com/losangeles/news/2017/04/05/forever-21-expanding-f21-red-concept.html.
C.S. Lewis College. "C.S. Lewis." Accessed June 27, 2018, http://www.cslewiscollege.org/c-s-lewis/.

Curan, Catherine. "Churches Are Now Accepting Donations Through Apps." *New York Post*. March 31, 2018. https://nypost.com/2018/03/31/churches-are-now-accepting-donations-through-apps/.

Daniels, David. "How Beautiful Eulogy United," Wade-O Radio. October 29, 2013. http://wadeoradio.com/beautiful-eulogy-united/.

Ericksen, Glenn. Interview by Phillip Reeves. May 2018.

Erlanger, Steven. "The Chronicles of C.S. Lewis Lead to Poets' Corner." *New York Times*. November 20, 2013. http://www.nytimes.com/2013/11/21/books/the-chronicles-ofc-s-lewis-lead-to-poets-corner.html?_r=0.

Ethics and Public Policy Center. "About." Accessed June 27, 2018. https://eppc.org/about/.

———. "Fellows and Scholars." Accessed June 27, 2018. https://eppc.org/authors-scholars/.

———. "Programs." Accessed June 27, 2018. https://eppc.org/programs/.

Exodus Cry, "About." Accessed June 24, 2018. https://exoduscry.com/about/.

Faith Angle Forum. "About." Accessed June 29, 2018. https://faithangle.org/about/.

Forbes. "Profile: Do Won & Jin Sook Chang." Accessed June 25, 2018. https://www.forbes.com/profile/do-won-jin-sook-chang/.

Horton, Scott. "Reporting on C Street." *Harper's*. August 17, 2009. https://harpers.org/blog/2009/08/reporting-on-c-street/.

Human Rights Watch. "Burma." Accessed June 28, 2018. https://www.hrw.org/asia/burma.

Humble Beast Records. "About." Accessed June 25, 2018. https://humblebeast.com/about/.

———. "Humble Beast Becomes More Than Music." Vimeo, ADD DATE. https://vimeo.com/218840942.

———. "Humble Beast Introduces Left Roasters." YouTube. January 8, 2015. https://www.youtube.com/watch?v=k25vpwNItxQ.

Hustek, Natalie. Discussion with author. June 2018.

Independence Hall Association. "The Presbyterian Historical Society." Accessed May 18, 2018. http://www.ushistory.org/tour/presbyterian-historical-society.htm.

International Justice Mission. "Get to Know Us." Accessed June 29, 2018. https://www.ijm.org/get-to-know-us.

———. "Slavery." Accessed June 29, 2018. https://www.ijm.org/slavery.

———. "Who We Are." Accessed June 29, 2018. https://www.ijm.org/who-we-are.

JSTOR. "Publisher Description: Presbyterian Historical Society." Accessed June 22, 2018. https://www.jstor.org/publisher/phs.

L'Abri. "History." Accessed June 26, 2018. http://labri.org/history.html.

Magic Lantern Pictures. "You've Seen Liberated: What's Next?" Accessed June 23, 2018. http://magiclanternpictures.org/liberated/.

McGregor, Jena. "Forever 21's Leaked Memo: Faith at Work?" *Washington Post*. August 19, 2013. https://www.washingtonpost.com/news/on-leadership/

wp/2013/08/19/forever-21s-leaked-memo-faith-at-work/?utm_term=.
ba03a70b5424.

Monda, Andrea. "The Conversion Story of C.S. Lewis." EWTN. July 16, 2008. http://www.ewtn.com/library/SPIRIT/cslewconv.htm.

Praxis Labs. "Our Vision." Accessed June 24, 2018. http://www.praxislabs.org/.

Presbyterian Historical Society. "About." Accessed May 18, 2018. https://www.history.pcusa.org/about.

————. "Exhibits." Accessed June 22, 2018. https://www.history.pcusa.org/history-online/exhibits.

————. "History Online." Accessed June 21, 2018. https://www.history.pcusa.org/history-online.

Presbyterian Historical Society of Ireland. "About Us." Accessed July 6, 2018. http://www.presbyterianhistoryireland.com/about-us/.

Smith, Nicola. "Burmese Soldiers Accused of Escalating Violence Against Northern Minorities." *Telegraph.* March 15, 2018. https://www.telegraph.co.uk/news/2018/03/15/burmese-soldiers-accused-escalating-violence-against-northern/.

Smith, Scott C. "C.S. Lewis Wrote Christian Novels that Became Global Best-Sellers." *Investor's Business Daily.* March 31, 2016. https://www.investors.com/news/management/leaders-and-success/c-s-lewis-wrote-christian-novels-that-became-global-best-sellers/.

Vincent, Alice E. "C.S. Lewis Facts: 11 Things You Never Knew About the Narnia Author." *Huffington Post.* November 29, 2012. https://www.huffingtonpost.co.uk/2012/11/29/cs-lewis-narnia-facts-_n_2209399.html.

Wise, Talia. "Netflix Teams with Christian Group to Tackle Toxic Sexual Norms Among Millenials." CBN News. January 31, 2018. http://www1.cbn.com/cbnnews/entertainment/2018/january/netflix-teams-up-with-christian-group-to-tackle-toxic-sexual-norms-among-millenials.

Wiseman, Eva. "The Gospel According to Forever 21." *Guardian.* July 16, 2011. https://www.theguardian.com/lifeandstyle/2011/jul/17/forever-21-fast-fashion-america.

World Atlas. "Which Countries Have the Most Christians." Accessed October 8, 2018. https://www.worldatlas.com/articles/which-countries-have-the-most-christians-around-the-world.html.

Worthen, Molly. "Not Your Father's L'Abri." *Christianity Today.* March 28, 2008. https://www.christianitytoday.com/ct/2008/march/36.60.html.